Sefer

TOMER DEVORAH

The Palm Tree of Deborah

תּוֹמֶר דְּבוֹרָה

לרמ"ק

Kabbalist Rabbi

Moshe Cordovero

The RaMaK

There is no known book without mistakes. Therefore, I ask in every language of application if anyone has any questions, comments, clarifications, corrections, please send to: **book@simchatchaim.com**

All material used in this section may not be used for commercial purposes, but only for study and teaching.

To get this book or books and information Email me at:

book@simchatchaim.com

Copyright©All Rights Reserved to

www.simchatchaim.com

YB"S©All rights reserved to the Editor

First Edition 2023

TABLE OF CONTENTS

Page	Contents
3	Rabbi Moshe Cordovero Z"L
5	Chapter One
37	Chapter Two
55	Chapter Three
63	Chapter Four
67	Chapter Five
81	Chapter Six
85	Chapter Seven
91	Chapter Eight
97	Chapter Nine
109	Chapter Ten

Cover page of a print 1558 Venice

Rabbi Moshe Cordovero Z"L

Moshe Cordovero, also referred to as Ra'MaK, was a leading kabbalist who lived and taught in Tsfat. His best-known work, Pardes Rimmonim, is a systematization of various school of kabbalistic thought. He authored many highly influential works, included a defense of kabbalah, a highly-regarded ethical work based on kabbalistic thought, and a comprehsive commentary on the Zohar. He had many disciples and was considered the premier kabbalistic authority until superceded by Rabbi Yitzchak Luria (AR"I Z"L) shortly after his death.

Rabbi Moses ben Jacob Cordovero was a central figure in the historical development of Kabbalah, leader of a mystical school in 16th-century Safed, Ottoman Syria. He is known by the acronym the Rama"k.

After the Medieval flourishing of Kabbalah, centered on the Zohar, attempts were made to give a complete intellectual system to its theology, such as by Meir ibn Gabbai. Influenced by the earlier success of Jewish philosophy in articulating a rational study of Jewish thought, Moshe Cordovero produced the first full integration of the previous differing schools in Kabbalistic interpretation. While he was a mystic inspired by the opaque imagery of the Zohar, Cordoverian Kabbalah utilised the conceptual framework of evolving cause and effect from the Infinite to the Finite in systemising Kabbalah, the method of philosophical style discourse he held most effective in describing a process that reflects sequential logic and coherence. His encyclopedic works became a central stage in the development of Kabbalah.

Immediately after him in Safed, Isaac Luria articulated a subsequent system of Kabbalistic theology, with new supra-rational doctrines recasting previous Kabbalistic thought. While Lurianism displaced the Cordoverian scheme and became predominant in Judaism, its followers read Cordoverian works in harmony with their teachings. Where to them, Lurianism described the "World" of Rectification, Cordovero described the pre-Rectification World.[3] Both articulations of the 16th century mystical Renaissance in Safed gave Kabbalah an intellectual prominence to rival Medieval Rationalism, whose social influence on Judaism had waned after the Expulsion from Spain.

Sefer Tomer Devorah

Chapter One

That it is fitting for a person to resemble his Creator:

It is fitting for a person to resemble his Creator and then he will be [configured] in the secret of the Highest Form, [both] in image and likeness. As if he is alike in his body but not in his actions, he betrays the Form; and they will say about him, "A lovely form, but ugly deeds." As behold, the essence of the Highest Image and Likeness is His actions. And what will it benefit him to have the structure of his limbs like the Highest Form, but not resemble his Creator in his actions? Therefore, it is fitting that he should [make his actions] resemble the actions of the Crown (Kete"r), which are the thirteen highest traits of mercy. And they are hinted to in the secret of the verses (Michah 7:18-20), "Who is a power like

You; He will again have mercy on us; You shall give truth." If so, it is fitting that these thirteen traits [also] be found in man. And now we will explain these thirteen actions that are fitting to be with him.

The First: "Who is a power like You"

instructs about the Holy One, blessed be He, being an insulted King [that] tolerates insult that is inconceivable. Behold, nothing is hidden from His oversight, without a doubt, and [yet] there is no moment when a person is not nourished and preserved by the Highest force that flows upon him; and behold, you find that there was never a person who sinned against God, without Him - at that very instant - [willing] the flow of his existence and the movement of his limbs. While this person sins with that force, He does not withhold it from him at all. Rather, the Holy One, blessed be He, tolerates such an insult - to flow the power for the movement of his limbs into the person, and the person [uses] that power at that moment for sin and iniquity, and [to] anger [Him];

and the Holy One, blessed be He, tolerates [it]. And you [should] not say that He is not able to withhold this goodness from him - God forbid. As behold, it is in His power to make his arms and legs rigid instantly, like His word - similar to what He did to Yerovam (I Kings 13:4). And even with all this, that He has the power in His hand to withdraw that flowing force, and He could have said, "Since you sin against Me, sin with your own [strength], not with Mine" - He does not withhold good from a person for this. Instead, He tolerates the insult, flows the force [to do this] and gives the person of His goodness. Behold, this is insult and [its] toleration that cannot be told. And for this, the ministering angels call the Holy One, blessed be He, the insulted King. And this is [the meaning of] its stating, "Who is a power like You" - You are a Power that is a Master of Kindness that benefits, a Power that is a Master of strength to take revenge and take back what is Yours; and with all that, You tolerate [it] and are insulted until [the person] repents.

Behold, this is a trait that a person must practice - I mean tolerance; and, so, to be insulted, even to this extent, and nonetheless not to withhold one's goodness from the recipient.

The second: "Who bears iniquity"

And behold, this is greater than the previous. As behold, a man does not do an iniquity without creating a destructive spirit (mashchit); as it is learned (Avot 4:11), "One who transgresses a single iniquity acquires a single prosecutor." And behold, this prosecutor stands in front of the Holy One, blessed be He, and says, "X made me." And no creature exists in the world except from the flow of the Holy One, blessed be He - and behold, this destructive spirit that stands in front of the Holy One, blessed be He, from what does he exist? It would be logical that the Holy One, blessed be He, would say, "I do not nourish destructive spirits - he should go to the one that made him and be sustained from him." And the destructive spirit would go down immediately and take his soul, excise him or have him punished according to his punishment - until this destructive spirit is nullified. But the Holy One, blessed be He, does not do this; but He rather bears and tolerates the iniquity - and [just] as He nourishes and sustains the whole world, [so too] does He nourish and sustain this destructive spirit until there be one of three things: Either the sinner repents and he finishes him and nullifies him with his mortifications; or that the righteous Judge nullifies him with afflictions and death; or [that the sinner] goes to Geihinom and he pays his debt there. And that is [the meaning of] that which Kain said (Genesis 4:13), "Is my iniquity too great to bear?" And the Sages, may their memory be blessed, explained it (Midrash Tanchuma, Bereshit 9), "You tolerate the whole world" - meaning nourish and sustain - "and my iniquity is [so] heavy that you cannot tolerate it" - meaning to sustain it until I repent and repair [it]. If so, behold this is a great trait of tolerance - that He nourishes and sustains an evil creature, that the sinner created, until he repents.

A person [should] learn [from this] how much he needs to be tolerant, to carry the yoke of his fellow and his evils that he did against him; to the measure such that his evil that he sinned against him is still in existence - and he tolerates [it] until his fellow repairs [it], or that it is nullified by itself, and similar to it.

The third: "And passes over transgression"

This is a great trait. As behold, the pardon is not through an emissary but rather actually through the Holy One, blessed be He - as it is written (Psalm 130:4), "For with You is forgiveness, etc." And what is that forgiveness? That He washes away the transgression, as it is written (Isaiah 4:4), "When the Lord will have washed away the filth of the daughters of Zion, etc." And so [too,] is it written (Ezekiel 36:25), "I will sprinkle upon you pure waters, etc." And this is [the meaning of] "and passes over transgression" - He sends forth waters of washing, and He passes and washes [away] the transgression.

And behold, just like this likeness must a person be - such that he not says, "And shall I fix what x sinned or destroyed?" He should not say like this; for behold, a person sins and the Holy One, blessed be He - Himself, and not through an emissary - 'fixes the twisted,' and washes away the filth of his transgression.

And from here, the person will be ashamed to sin again; for behold, the King, Himself, washes the dirt of his clothes.

The fourth - "To the remnant of His inheritance"

Behold, the Holy One, blessed be He, acts with His people in this way, to say, "What can I do with Israel, [as] they are My relatives - relation of flesh do I have with them." As they are the spouse to the Holy One, blessed be He; and He calls them, "My daughter" and "My sister," "My Mother" - as they, may their memory be blessed, explained (Shir HaShirim Rabbah 3:11:2). And it is written (Psalms 148:14), "Israel, His close (kerovo) nation" - He has actual closeness (kurvah) with them, and they are His children. And that is [the meaning of] the remnant of (she'erit) His inheritance" - it is an expression of relation (she'er) of flesh; and in the end, they are His (literal) inheritance. "And what shall I say? If I punish them, behold the pain is upon Me; as it is written (Isaiah 63:9), 'In all their distress, the distress (tsar) was to Him.'" And [to Him (lo)] is written with a [letter,] alef, to say that their pain reached the Highest Wonder (Wonder, peleh, being composed of the same letters as the spelling of alef, and representing Kete"r) - and all the more so, the two Faces through which is the central running [of the world] - but it is written with a [letter,] vav, [to mean that] the distress is to Him. And it is written (Judges 10:16), "and His soul could not bear the travail of Israel" - as He does not bear their pain and their disgrace, because they are "the she'erit [of] His inheritance."

So is it [regarding] a man with his fellow: All Israel are relations of flesh, these with those. Since all of their souls are bound together, this one has a share in that and that one has a share in this. And hence it is not similar when the many do the commandments [to when they are only done by individuals]. And all of this is because of their being bound together. And our Rabbis, may their memory be blessed, thus explained (Berakhot 47b) about the one who is counted from the first ten in the synagogue - [that] even if a hundred come after him, he recieves the reward that corresponds to all of them. It is actually a hundred, as per its understanding. Since the ten are included - these in those - behold, they are ten times ten, one hundred. And [so] each one of them is composed of a hundred [parts]. If so, even if one hundred come [afterwards], he has the reward of a hundred. As so from this reason, Israel are guarantors for each other. Since each one actually has a part of his fellow - when the one sins, he damages himself and he damages the part that his fellow has in him. It comes out from the side of that part that his fellow is his guarantor. If so, they are the relation, one of the other. And hence it is fitting that a person be desiring of the good of his fellow and his eye be good towards the good of his fellow, and that his honor should be as beloved to him as his [own] - as he is literally him[self]. And from this reason were we commanded (Leviticus 19:18), "you shall love your neighbor as yourself." And it is fitting that he desires the propriety of his fellow and not speak about his disgrace at all. And he [should] not want it, in the way that the Holy One, blessed be He, does not want our disgrace nor our pain - from the reason of relation. So too [should] he not want the disgrace of his fellow nor his pain, nor his corruption. And it [should] be bad for him on account of [his fellow], as if he was actually experiencing that pain, or [good for him from] that good [that he experiences].

The fifth - "He does not hold on to His fury forever"

This is a different trait: that even if a person holds on to his sin, the Holy One, blessed be He, does not hold on to His fury. And if He holds on to it, not forever. Rather, He nullifies His anger, even if the person does not repent. As we found in the days of Yerovam the son of Yoash, that the Holy One, blessed be He, brought back the boundary of Israel [from occupation] and they were [still] worshipping calves - He had mercy upon them, but they did not repent. If so, why did He have mercy? For the sake of this trait, that He does not hold on to his fury forever. Just the opposite, His fury weakens - even as the sin is still in existence, He does not punish, but rather He expects and has mercy that they may repent. And that is [the meaning of] "He will not contend forever, or begrudge for all time" (Psalms 103:9). Rather, the Holy One, blessed be He, acts with softnesses and harshnesses, all for the good of Israel.

And this is a trait that is fitting for a person to practice with his fellow. Even if he is permitted to rebuke his fellow or his sons with upbraiding and they [accept it], it is not because of this that he [should] increase his rebuke. And he [should] not hold on to his anger - even if he got angry - but rather nullify it. And he [should] not hold on to his rage forever, even if it is a [rage] that is permitted to a person, similar to that which they explained:

"When you see the donkey of your fellow, etc." (Exodus 23:5); and they explained (Pesachim 113b) what is this anger - that he saw him transgressing a sin, but [the one seeing] is [alone, such that] he may not testify; and [so] he hates him for the matter of the sin. And even so, the Torah states, "you shall surely release with him" - leave that which is in your heart; rather it is a commandment to bring him close with love. [As] perhaps it will be beneficial [to act] in this way. And this is exactly the trait of, "He does not hold on to His fury forever."

The sixth: "For He is One that desires kindness"

Did we not already explain in its place that in the known chamber, there are angels appointed to receive the bestowing of kindness that a man does in this world? And when the trait of justice prosecutes against Israel, these angels immediately show this kindness, and the Holy One, blessed be He, has mercy upon Israel, since He desires kindness. And even with their being liable, if they bestow kindness - this one to that one - He has mercy upon them. And it is like it was at the time of the destruction [of the Temple]: That it was told to Gavriel (Ezekiel 10:2), "Go inside the wheelwork, etc." - as he is the minister of judgement and power; and He gave him authority to receive powers of judgement, inside the wheelwork from under the cherubs, from the fire of the altar. This is the judgement of the power of kingship (malkhut). And the judgement was intensified until it sought to finish everything off - to uproot the seed of Israel, since they were liable for destruction. And it is written (Ezekiel 10:8), "And by the cherubs there appeared the form of the hand of a man under their wings." And this is [meaning] that the Holy One, blessed be He, said to Gavriel, "They are bestowing acts of kindness - these with those - and even if they are liable, they are saved and there shall be a remnant from them." And the reason is because of this trait - since He is One who desires kindness, He desires that which Israel does kindness. And He recalls that side for them, even as they are not fitting from another side.

If so, it is fitting for a person to practice this approach. If he sees a person doing evil to him and angering him - if there is a good side to [that person], that he does good to others or [has] a good trait that he practice appropriately, that side should suffice for him to nullify his anger from upon him. And his heart [should] be appeased about him; and he [should] desire kindness and say, "It is enough for me with this goodness that he has." And all the more so [is this the case] with his wife; as our Rabbis explained (Yevamot 63a), "It is enough that they raise our children, and save us from sin." So should he say about every person, "It is enough for me with x goodness that he did for me," or "that he did with y," or "[with the] good trait z that he has." He will [hence] be desiring kindness.

The seventh: "He will again have mercy on us"

behold, the Holy One, blessed be He, does not follow the trait of flesh and blood. [That trait is that] if [someone] angers him - if he is appeased from him, he is a little appeased, [but] not like the previous love [he had for him]. But if a person sinned [to God] and he repents, his stature is greater with the Holy One, blessed be He, [than before]. And this is [the meaning of] "In the place that penitents stand, [even] completely righteous ones cannot stand" (Berakhot 34b). And the reason is like they explained in the chapter [entitled] HaBoneh (it is in Menachot 29b in our texts) regarding why [the letter,] hey is made like a portico: "Such that the one that wants to exit from his world [may] exit." The explanation is that the world was created with a hey. And the Holy One, blessed be He, created the world widely open to the side of evil and sin. There is no side that does not have physicality, the evil impulse and defect - like a type of portico. It does not have fences but rather has a large breach, open towards the side of evil, to the bottom side. How many openings are there for anyone who wants to exit from his world - he cannot turn to a side that he will not find a side of sin and iniquity to go out to the external forces (chitsonim)! But it is [also] open from above; so that if he repents, he will be accepted. And they asked, "Let him be taken back through [the bottom]!" [They answered,] "the matter will not help." They [meant] with this that one who repents will not suffice to be fenced from iniquity [with a fence] like the fence of the righteous ones that did not sin - a small fence suffices for them. However, a small fence will not suffice for the sinner that sinned and repented. Rather, he needs to fence himself with several difficult fences, since he already breached the small fence once. If he approaches there, his impulse seduces him easily. Rather he needs to distance himself with a very great distancing. And for this [reason], he does not enter through the opening of the portico, where the breach is there. Rather, he ascends and enters through the small opening, [such that] he makes several difficulties and mortifications for himself and [thereby] closes the breaches.

And from this reason, "In the place that penitents stand, etc." - because they do not enter through the opening of the righteous ones, so that they will be with the righteous ones. Rather, they trudge and climb through the higher opening, and mortify themselves and become much more separated from sin than the righteous ones. Hence, they climbed and stood on the level of hay (the numerical equivalent of which is five) - the fifth chamber in the Garden of Eden, which is the roof of the hey - whereas the righteous ones are at the opening of the hey, at the entrance of the portico. And accordingly, when a person undergoes repentance (teshuvah) - which is [that] hey returns (teshuv hey) to its place - and the Holy One, blessed be He, brings back His Presence upon him, He does not come back [with a love] only like the first love, but rather much more. And this is [the meaning of] "He will again have mercy on us" - that He will add to His mercy on Israel and refine them more and bring them closer.

And so, must a person act towards his fellow. He should not begrudge enmity from the earlier anger. But rather when he sees that his fellow seeks his love, he should have a level of mercy and love [that is] much more than before. And he should say, "Behold, for me he is like penitents, that the completely righteous cannot stand next to them." And he [should] bring him the closest - closer than he brings those that are completely righteous with him, that have not sinned towards him.

The eighth: "He suppresses our iniquities"

Behold, the Holy One, blessed be He, acts with Israel with this trait, and that is the secret of the suppression of iniquities. As behold the commandment, 'it is like when it blossoms, its bud arises' and it pierces and climbs until no end, to enter in front of Him, may He be blessed. But the iniquities, however, do not have passage there, God forbid. Rather, He suppresses them, such that they not enter - as it is written (Psalms 5:5), "evil does not dwell [with] You (yegurcha)"; evil shall not dwell in Your domicile (megurcha). If so, the iniquity does not enter inside. And from this reason, "There is no reward for a commandment in this world" (Kiddushin 39a) - as [the commandments] are in front of Him, may He be blessed. And how can He give him from that which is in front of Him - a spiritual reward - in the world that is physical? And behold, the entire world is not worth one commandment and the satisfaction [from it] in front of Him. And for this reason, He does not take the bribe of commandments. The metaphor for this is that the Holy One, blessed be He, does not say, "He did forty commandments and ten sins; there remain thirty and the [other] ten go [away] with the ten" - God forbid! Rather, even if he was a completely righteous one and he committed one sin, it is similar in front of Him as if he burned the entire Torah, until he satisfies his debt. And afterwards, he can receive the reward for all of his commandments. And this is a great kindness that the Holy One, blessed be He, does with the righteous ones - that he does not reduce [the reward], as the commandments are very important and climb until [they reach] in front of Him, may He be blessed. And how could He reduce from them on account of sins - as the repayment of sins is from the share of Geihinom, from that which is disdained; whereas the reward of the commandments is from the honored, the radiance of the Divine Presence. How could these be reduced [on account of] those? Rather, the Holy One, blessed be He, collects the debt of the sins and pays the reward of all of the commandments. And this is [the meaning of] "He suppresses our iniquities" - that the iniquities do not intensify in front of Him, like the commandments. Rather He suppresses them that they should not rise and not enter - even as He is supervising over the ways of a man, good and bad. Nonetheless, He does not suppress the good, but rather it blossoms and climbs until [it grows] very much. And [so] one commandment is grouped together with [another] commandment and a great edifice is built, and a fine suit [is formed]. But iniquities do not have this special quality, but He rather suppresses them, that they should not have this success, and [not] enter inside [in front of Him].

A man needs to also practice this trait - to not suppress the good of his fellow and remember his evil that he did to him. Rather, just the opposite - he [should] suppress the evil, forget it and neglect it, and 'evil shall not dwell in his domicile.' And the good [should] always be ordered in front of him, and he [should] remember [his fellow's] good. And he [should] intensify it over all of the deeds that he has done to him. And he [should] not reduce [that] in his heart, and say, "If he did me good, behold he [also] did me evil," and forget the good. He should not do this. Rather, he [should] be appeased in any way of appeasement [possible]. And he [should] never neglect the good from [being] between his eyes; and avert his eye from the evil as much as he can, in the way that the Holy One, blessed be He, suppresses His iniquities, as I have explained.

The ninth: "And You will hurl into the depths of the sea all of their sins"

This is a good trait of the Holy One, blessed be He. As behold, Israel sinned; He delivered them into the hand of Pharaoh, and they repented. Why [should] he punish Pharaoh? And likewise,

Sancheriv; and likewise, Haman and those similar to them. The Holy One, blessed be He, is not only assuaged to say, "They have repented. If so, let them not have any more evil. If so, let Haman withdraw from them," or Pharaoh, or Sancheriv. This does not suffice. Rather, he puts the travail of Haman back on his head; and likewise, Pharaoh; and likewise, Sancheriv. And the reason for this practice is the secret of "And the goat carries upon him all of their iniquities to a desolate land" (Leviticus 16:22). And its explanation is that it carries the actual sins. But this is very difficult: And shall Israel sin and the goat carry [it]? Rather [this] trait is like this: A person confesses [sins], and his intention in the confession is to receive purification upon himself; like the matter that David stated (Psalms 51:4), "Wash me thoroughly from my iniquity." And so, in our saying, "Purge [me] in Your great mercy," [one] is only praying that the afflictions be light, such that there not be a hindrance of Torah [study]; and this [is also the intention of] that which we say, "But not through bad (harsh) afflictions." And so, in his saying, "And You are righteous about all that happens to me" - he intends to truly accept afflictions with a pleasant countenance, in order to atone; as there are iniquities that [only] afflictions purge or that [only] death purges. And such is the trait: As soon as this one confesses in his prayer - they explained in the Zohar in Parshat Pekudei (p. 262b) that this is the portion of Samael, similar to the goat. What is his portion that the Holy One, blessed be He, decreed for him? Afflictions. And [so] Samael immediately arrives there and goes and collects his debt. And behold, [this is] the goat carrying the iniquities - that the Holy One, blessed be He, gives him authority to collect his debt, and Israel is [thus] purified. But, behold, it all devolves upon Samael. And the reason is because the Holy One, blessed be He, decreed upon His world, that anyone who does this, will be nullified. And this is the reason of, "and you shall kill the beast" (Leviticus 20:15). And likewise, the stone of the commandment of those stoned; and the sword of the commandment of those killed, require burial (Sanhedrin 45b) to nullify their existence and power after their judgement is finished.

And behold, there is actually the secret of the image of Nevuchadnetsar in this: Israel was given over to the hand of the king of Babylonia, "the head of gold" (Daniel 2:32). That head was humbled and given over to the hand of Persia, who are "the chest and the arms of silver." And likewise, these were pushed off for those, until Israel descended to "their feet, some of them were iron and some of them were clay" (Daniel 2:33). And what is the good finish? In the end, the Holy One, blessed be He, stands them up and carries out judgement upon them, as it is written (Deuteronomy 32:23), "I will finish My arrows upon them" - My arrows end, but Israel does not end (Sotah 9a). "All at once, the (bronze, silver, gold, etc.) were crushed" (Daniel 2:35). Behold at the beginning, it is written (Daniel 2:34), "and struck the image on its feet" - there is nothing of the image besides its feet, as the power of the head, its arms and its belly had already been nullified. And nonetheless at the end, it was crushed [entirely] as one. In the future, the Holy One, blessed be He, will stand up Samael and the evildoers that do his deeds and acts, and carry out the judgement upon them. And that is [the meaning of] "and You will hurl into the depths of the sea all of their sins" - it wants [to say], He will hurl the power of judgement to bring [it] down on the hands of these, who are "the depths of the sea." [As it is stated (Isaiah 57:20),] "But the wicked are like the troubled sea which cannot rest, whose waters toss up mire and mud" - these are the ones that enact judgement upon Israel, all the payment of whom falls back on their heads. And the reason is because after Israel has received their judgement, the Holy One, blessed be He, regrets even about what preceded, and He [avenges] their insult. And it is not enough [that they carried out the judgement on Israel], but rather, "I was a little mad, but they assisted for the bad" (Zechariah 1:15).

Also, this trait must a person practice with his fellow. Even if he is an evildoer that is plagued with afflictions, he shall not hate him - as once he has been debased, behold he is like your brother (Makkot 23a). And he [should] bring close the downtrodden and punished and have mercy upon them. And just the opposite, he should save them from the hand of the enemy, and he should not say, "It is his iniquity that caused it to him." But rather, he should have mercy upon him with this trait, as I have explained.

The tenth: "You shall give truth to Yaakov"

This trait is that Israel has a virtue. Those average people that do not know how to act beyond the [letter] of the law - and they are called Yaakov, since they only act with true behavior; and also the Holy One, blessed be He, has a trait of truth, which is from the angle of the existence of straight judgement. And with these who act with straightness in the world, the Holy One, blessed be He, acts with truth. He has mercy upon them from the angle of straightness and judgement.

A person must also behave with his fellow from the angle of straightness and truth, without inclining the judgement of his fellow - to have mercy upon him in truth; [just] like God, may He be blessed, has mercy upon the average creatures with the trait of truth [in order] to refine them.

The eleventh: "Kindness to Avraham"

These are the ones that act beyond the [letter] of the law in the world, like Avraham, our father; also, the Holy One, blessed be He, acts with them beyond the [letter] of the law. He does not take the law (judgement) to its [full] force, even in the way of straightness. Rather, He [seeks to] go beyond straightness with them, [just] like they act. And that is [the meaning of] "kindness to Avraham" - the Holy One, blessed be He, practices the trait of kindness with those that are like Avraham in their behavior.

Also, a person even as he acts with righteousness, straightness and justice towards every person - his behavior towards the best and the pious [should] be beyond the [letter] of the law. And if he was a little patient with other people - towards these [he should be] much more [patient], and have mercy upon them; to go with them beyond the [letter] of the law that he follows with all other people. And these must be very, very important in front of him and [be] beloved to him. And they [should] be from the people of his entourage.

The twelfth: "Which You swore to our fathers"

There are people that are not proper, and the Holy One, blessed be He, has mercy on all of them. And they explained in the Gemara (Berakhot 7a), "and I will give grace to the one that I give grace" (Exodus 33:19) - "The Holy One, blessed be He, said, 'This storehouse is for those that are not proper.'" There is a storehouse of those given grace that the Holy One, blessed be He, graces and gives them [as] a free present. As the Holy One, blessed be He, said, "Behold, they have the merit of the fathers - I swore to the fathers. Therefore, even if they are not proper, they shall merit because they are from the seed of the fathers to whom I swore. Hence, I will lead them and guide them until they are refined."

And so, should a person be if he meets evildoers: He should not be cruel towards them or curse them and similar [to these things]. Rather, he should have mercy upon them and say, "In the end, they are the children of Avraham, Yitschak and Yaakov. If they are not fit, their fathers were fit and proper. And one who disgraces the children, disgraces the fathers. [Hence] I do not desire that they be disgraced through me." And he covers their insult and refines them according to his ability.

The thirteenth: "From days of yore"

Behold [this is] the trait that the Holy One, blessed be He, has with Israel when their merit and similar [to it] ends. What shall He do - behold, they are not proper in their own right? It is written (Jeremiah 2:2), "I remembered for you the kindness of your youth, your love as a bride" - the Holy One, blessed be He, actually remembers the days of the early ones, the love that He had from before, and has mercy upon Israel. And through this, He remembers for them all the commandments that they did from the day they were born and all of the good traits with which the Holy One, blessed be He, runs His world. And from all of them, He produces a special quality to have mercy for them. And behold, this trait includes all of the traits entirely, as they explained in the Idra (Zohar, Nasso, p. 134b).

So [should] a person refines his behavior with people, such that even if he does not find an argument from those mentioned [in the other traits], he should say, "There were already times when they did not sin. And behold, that time, or those earlier days, they were fit." And he [should] remember for them that good that they did in their childhood, and remember for them the love of the 'ones weaned from milk, removed from the breasts.' And through this, there will not be a man who will not be fit to benefit, to pray for his welfare and to have mercy upon him.

To now [we] have reached the thirteen traits though which a person should resemble his Creator, which are the highest traits of mercy. And their special quality is that [just] as a person acts below, so [too] will he merit to open for himself the highest trait above - exactly as he acts, so will there be a flow from above. And he will cause that trait to shine in the world. And so, he should not have these thirteen traits escape from the eyes of [his] mind. And he [should] not stop the verse from his mouth, so that it will be a reminder - when a situation comes to him that he needs to uses one of the traits, he will remember and say, "Behold, that thing depends upon trait x; I do not want to move from it, so that this trait does not disappear and retreat from the world."

TOMER　　　Chapter One　　　DEVORAH

Sefer Tomer Devorah

Chapter Two

Some major activities that are the main governance:

Further for a person to resemble his Creator from the secret of the trait of the Crown (Kete"r), he must [do] some major activities - which are the main governance.

The first:

The trait of humility which includes everything - because it is dependent on the Crown. As behold, it is a trait over all of the Traits, but it does not raise itself and become proud above [the others]. Indeed, it goes down and always looks downwards. And that is from two reasons: The one is that It is embarrassed to look at Its Cause, rather Its Emanator always looks down upon It to benefit It; and It looks down to the lower ones. So [too,] must a person be embarrassed from staring upwards, to be proud. Rather, he must always stare downwards, to diminish himself all that he can. And behold, this trait is generally dependent upon the head of a man. As a man only shows his pride with the lifting of his head upwards, whereas the poor person lowers his head downwards. And behold, there is none as tolerant and humble as our God with the trait of the Crown, such that He is the epitome of mercy. And there is no defect nor iniquity nor judgement nor any other trait that intervenes in front of Him, that prevents [Him] from surveying, flowing and bestowing good constantly. So must a person [be], that no cause in the world prevent him from bestowing good; and that no iniquity or improper act of people intervene in front of him in order to impede him from bestowing good from those that need his good at any time and at any instant. And [just] like He sits and nourishes 'from the antelope's horns to the lice's eggs,' and does not disgrace any creature - as if He were to disgrace the creatures because of their smallness, they would not exist in the world even for an instant - but [He] rather supervises and gives His mercies upon them all; so must a man be, to bestow good to all and not to have any creature disgraced in front of him. Rather, even the puniest of the puny creatures [should] be very important in his eyes, and he [should] put his mind to it; and bestow good to all that need his good. And this trait is dependent on the Crown, in the secret of the Head as a whole.

The second:

That his thought resembles the thought of the Crown. [Just] as that Wisdom (Chochma"h) does not ever cease to think good thoughts and evil does not intervene - as It is complete mercy, and there is no judgment there, nor any hardness at all - so [should] a man's thought be always free from anything ugly. And [just] as It is the secret of the Wisdom of the primordial Torah and It is never lacking the secret of the Torah; so must he not divert himself to any diversion from the thought of Torah and [from] thinking about the greatness of God and His good actions, bestowing good, and similar to this.

The principle of the thing is that no foreign or idle thing should intervene in his thought. And this was the virtue of Rabbi Shimon (bar Yochai) and his colleagues - and behold in the Zohar in Parshat Vayakhel, how much Rabbi Shimon chastised Rabbi Yose when he diverted his thought a little.

The third:

That there not be any hardness in his forehead at all, but it rather resembles the Forehead of will, that wills everything. Even if he finds people angering [him], he [should] appease them and quiet them with his good will. As so is the will of the Forehead - always willing, appeasing the severities (gevurot) and refining them. So [too, should] he appeases the powerful ones (geeborim) that intensify their anger; and he [should] lead them with good will and engulf [them] with great wisdom to quiet the anger - so that it not passes the limit and be destructive,

God forbid. And he [should] use the model of the Higher Will, which is drawn from the wondrous Wisdom of the Forehead of the Ancient One (Aatika), and appeases all from there.

And he [should] draw [on this] to always be agreeable towards the creatures; as if his traits are hard with people from a [particular] angle, they will not be appeased by him. And this is the explanation of the mishnah (Avot 3:10), "Anyone from whom the spirit of creations find pleasure, from him the spirit of the Omnipresent finds pleasure."

The fourth:

That his ears are always inclined to hear the good. Indeed, a useless or disgraceful report [should] not enter them at all. In the way that no yelling of judgement nor defect of evil speech enters the Highest Listening, so [should] he only listens to goodnesses and beneficial things. And he [should] not listen to the other things that intensify anger at all. And [just] like the snake, his speech and his expression do not enter Above, so [too,] must no disgraceful thing enter to him. And that is [the meaning of, "You shall not raise a false report" (Exodus 23:1) - all the more so, [should] the other disgraceful things not enter his ear at all. And it [should] only listen to good things.

The fifth:

His eyes [should] not gaze at any disgraceful thing at all. Indeed, they [should] always be open to survey and have mercy upon all the despondent, according to his ability. And when he sees the distress of a poor person, he [should] not shut his eyes at all. Rather, he [should] contemplate about him in his mind - according to his ability - and arouse mercy upon him in front of the Heavens and in front of the creatures. And he [should] distance himself from all observation of evil, in the way that the Highest Eye is open and gazes immediately at the good.

The sixth:

That there [should] never be burning fury (literally, fury of the nose) from his nostril at all.

Rather, that there always be life, good will and patience (literally, duration of nose) in his nose. And he [should] always want to fulfill the will [of others], to satisfy every request and to sustain every downtrodden one; and always extract forgiveness of iniquity and (stopping) [passing over] of transgression from his [breath]. And he [should] not get angry with one who sins against him, but rather always be appeased and desire kindness, to create a pleasantness of spirit for all.

The seventh:

His face [should] always be shining and he [should] receive every person with a pleasant countenance. As so it is stated about the Highest Crown, "There is life in the light of the face of the King" (Proverbs 16:15); and no redness (harshness) or judgement enters there at all. So [should] the light of his face not be changed; anyone who gazes at him will only find joy and a pleasant countenance. And no cause [should] disrupt him from this at all.

The eighth:

His mouth [should] only bring out good; and the crafting of his statements be Torah and the causation of good will. And he [should] not bring out a disgraceful thing, a curse or the fury of anger from his mouth at all. And he [should] be similar to that Highest Mouth that never closes at all, and never prevents the good. And therefore, he must not be silent from speaking good about everything, and to always bring out goodness and blessing from this mouth.

Behold, these are eight good traits; and they are all under the masthead of humility. As they are above in the Crown, in the Highest Limbs. And at the time that a person wants to approach the Above, to resemble Him - to open his sources to those below - he must attain perfection in these two chapters.

When he must practice the traits of the Crown:

Indeed, we know that it is impossible to always practice these traits, as there are other traits in which a person must attain perfection - and those are the lower severities (gevuro"t), as we will elucidate. However, there are specific days that the severities are not active and people do not need them, as the Crown rules over them [then]; and times that the Crown is [wholly] required. Then one must use all of these traits that we mentioned.

Yet [with] the other traits - even if they are a need of the service at their [appropriate] times - [the times just mentioned are] not the time to use them, as the light of the Crown [would] nullify them; and hence he should not use those hard traits. For example, he [should] not use these traits on Shabbat - when the world is refined with the secret of delight, and [so] we do not judge [cases] on Shabbat. Then he [should] use all of these traits [of the Crown] - to open the Highest Sources. As if he focuses his concentration on the lights of the Crown in his prayers but he acts the opposite with his actions, how will he open the Source of the Crown? And behold, he actually pushes It off with his actions. And behold the things are an a fortiori argument (kal vechomer): If the Crown does not dwell in the Highest Sefirot (divine emanations) that intensify holy judgments and holy anger, is it not even more so that the Crown and Its light will not dwell upon a person who is intensifying external anger - even if it is for the sake of the Heavens? And even more so, since he comes to challenge the Highest Traits. And They [will] say, "How brazen-faced is that one - the light of the Crown is not revealed in Us because of Our holy and pure judgement, and he seeks to reveal It [while] he is full of anger and disgraceful external actions?"

Therefore, on holidays and Shabbat and Yom Kippur and at the time of prayer and the times of Torah involvement - that are [all] not times of severities, but rather times of the revelation of the Highest Will - a person must arrange his characteristics around all of these traits. And he can use the remaining traits for the service of God at the other times - but not the disgraceful one of them, as there is no time that it controls a person that it is not bad for him. And when he uses these traits [of the Crown], he can be prepared and sure that he will open the Highest Sources. Hence every man must gradually accustom himself to these traits. And the central one that he [should] grasp - which is the key to everything - is humility; as it is the head of all of them. It is the first aspect of the Crown, and all are included under it.

And behold, the essence of humility is that he not find any value at all in himself, but rather think of himself as nothing. And the matter is like the statement (Exodus 16:7), "and what are we, that you complain about us" - until he is in his eyes, the lowliest of all the creatures and very disgraceful and disgusting. And when he constantly toils to reach this trait, all the other traits will be dragged after it. As behold, the first trait that is in the Crown is that It makes Itself appear like nothing in front of Its Emanator. Likewise, [should] a person make himself [to be an] actual nothing; and he [should] think of his disappearance, as much better than his existence. And with this, he will be in front of his detractors as if the [truth] is with them and he is [actually] disgraceful and to be blamed. And this will be a catalyst for the acquisition of the good traits.

Suggestions to accustom oneself to humility:

And I have found a remedy for a person to gradually accustom himself to these things. It is possible that, through them, he will heal himself from the sickness of pride and enter the gates of humility. And it is a bandage made of three drugs.

The first:

That he accustoms himself to flee as much as he can from honor. As if he accustoms himself to having people honor him, he will become habituated from them towards the side of pride. And nature will make him want this always, and he can only be healed with difficulty.

The second:

That he accustoms his thought to see his disgrace and say, "If it is that people do not know of my inferiority, what is that to me? And do I, myself, not recognize that I am disgraceful with such and such" - whether it is with the lack of knowledge, the weakness of ability or the disgrace of food and the feces that come out from it, and similar to this - until he be disgraced in his eyes and disgusting.

The third:

That he constantly thinks about his iniquities and desire purification, upbraiding and afflictions. And he [should] say, "What are the best afflictions in the world, which will not disturb me from the service of God?" There is nothing more beloved in all of them than that they should curse him, and disgrace him and condemn him. As behold, they do not prevent him from his strength and vitality with sicknesses; and they do not prevent his eating and his clothing; and they do prevent his life and the life of his children with death. If so, he [should] truly want them and say, "What is it for me to fast and mortify myself with sackcloth and lashes - that weaken my strength from the service of God - that I should take them with my hand? It is better for me to mortify myself with the disgrace of people and their cursing me; and my strength will not depart and I will not be weakened." And with this, when insults come upon him, he will rejoice about them; and just the opposite, he will desire them. And he [should] make a bandage for his heart from these three drugs and train himself with it all of his days.

Additional suggestions to accustom oneself to humility:

And I have found a very good potion, but the potion does not help as much as the bandage mentioned above. And it is that he accustoms himself to two things.

The first:

It is to completely honor all of the creatures. Since he recognizes the virtue of the Creator that created man with wisdom - and the wisdom of the Creator is likewise in all of the creatures - and he, himself, sees that they are very, very honored; as the Creator of all, the virtuous Wise One, dealt with them in their creation. And if he disgraces them, God forbid, he touches on the honor of their Creator. And behold, this is similar to a wise smith - he made a vessel with great wisdom and he showed his creation to people. And one of them began to denounce it and to disgrace it. How much anger will come to that wise one - since they are disgracing his wisdom, in that they are disgracing the work of his hands. And so, too, will it be bad in the eyes of the Holy One, blessed be He, if they disgrace any creation of His creations. And this is [the meaning of] that which is written (Psalms 104:24), "How many are Your creations, Lord" - it does not state, "great," but rather, "many (rab"u)", an expression [like], "the important one (ra"v) of the house" (Esther 1:8), [meaning] they are very important - "You made all of them with wisdom": And since Your wisdom has been involved with them, Your works become important and great. And [so,] it is fitting for a person to contemplate wisdom in them, not disgrace.

TOMER — Chapter Two — DEVORAH

The second:

He [should] accustom himself to internalize the love of people into his heart - and even the evildoers - as if they were his brothers, and even more than this; until he fixes the love of all people into his heart. And he [should] even love the evildoers in his heart and say, "Who will give that they all be righteous penitents, and all be great ones and desirable to the Omnipresent," like the statement of the trusted friend of all of Israel. He stated (Numbers 11:29), "and who will give that all of the people of the Lord be prophets, etc?" And with what (how) will he love [them]? When he mentions in his thought the good [qualities] that they have and covers their blemish, and he not gaze at their scabs but rather at the good traits that they have. And he [should] say in his heart, "If this disgusting poor man was a man of much money, how happy I would be with his friendship - as I am with the friendship of x. And behold, if they would dress this one with nice clothes like x, behold there is no difference between them. If so, why [should] he lacks honor in my eyes? And behold, in the eyes of God, he is more important than I - as he is stricken and downtrodden with poverty and afflictions, and [so] cleaned of iniquity. And why would I hate one that the Holy One, blessed be He, loves?" And through this, his heart will turn to the side of the good and accustom himself to think about all the good traits that we mentioned.

TOMER Chapter Two DEVORAH

Sefer Tomer Devorah

Chapter Three

How a person can accustom himself with the trait of wisdom (chokhmah):

Behold, the Highest Wisdom is completely spread over all things that exist, even as It is very concealed and sublime. About It is it stated (Psalms 104:24), "How many are Your creations, Lord; You made all of them with wisdom." So [too,] is it fitting for a person's wisdom to be found in everything; and he [should] 'teach to benefit' people - he [should] endow each and every one according to his ability, that which he can endow from his wisdom. And no cause [should] disturb him [in this] at all.

The two sides of Wisdom:

And behold there are two sides to Wisdom.

The higher side that faces the Crown - that side does not gaze below, but rather receives from Above.

The second lower side that faces below - to survey the Sefirot that it extends to with its Wisdom.

So [should] there be two sides to a person.

The first side - that is meditation about his Creator in order to add to his wisdom and to refine it.

The second - to teach people from that wisdom that the Holy One, blessed be He, endowed upon him.

And [just] like Wisdom endows each and every Sefirah according to its size and need, he [should] endow [wisdom] to every person according to the measure of his intellect with which he can hold [it], and that which is pleasant for him and his need. And he [should] guard from giving more than the measure of the intellect of the endowed, so that a mishap not follow from it. As so is it that the higher Sefirah does not add beyond the restricted measure of the Receiver.

Surveillance over the needs of others:

It is also from the way of Wisdom for It to be surveying all things in existence, since It is the Thought that thinks about all things in existence. And about It is it stated (Isaiah 55:8), "For My thoughts are not your thoughts"; and written (II Samuel 14:14), "and He thinks thoughts that one banished not be banished from Him"; and [also] written (Jeremiah 29:11), "For I have known the thoughts that I am thinking about you, House of Israel; thoughts of peace, and not of evil, to give to you an ending of hope." So [too,] must a person's eyes be open over the behavior of the people of God, to benefit them. And his thoughts [should] be to bring close the banished, and to think good thoughts about them. [Just] like the Mind thinks [about the] benefit of all existence, so [should] he thinks about the benefit of his fellows and counsel them [with] advice [that is] good with God and with His people, [both] individually and generally. And he [should] lead one who leaves good behavior, towards straight behavior; and he [should] be like a mind and thought to steer him and lead him to good and straight action - [just] like the Highest Thought straightens the Highest Man (the Divine Emanations below It).

To bestow life. And Wisdom also gives life to everything, as it is written (Ecclesiastes 7:12), "and Wisdom gives life to the one that possesses It." So [too, should] he instructs life to the whole world and cause [them to have] life in this world and in the world to come, and facilitate life for them. This is the general principle - he [should] exude life for all.

To be like a father:

And Wisdom is also a Father to all that exist, as it is written (Psalms 104:24), "How many are Your creations, Lord; You made all of them with wisdom" - and they are living and survive from There. So [too,] must he be a father to all of the creations of the Holy One, blessed be He, and to

Israel, the essence - as they are the holy souls emanated from There. And he [should] always seek mercy and blessing for the world - in the way that the Highest Father is a Merciful One upon His creatures - and always pray about the distress of those in distress, as if they were his actual children and as if he created them. As this is the will of the Holy One, blessed be He - in the way that the faithful shepherd stated (Numbers 11:12), "Did I conceive all this people, that You should say to me, 'Carry them in your bosom.'" And in this [way], he [should] carry all of the people of God 'as a nurse carries an infant' - 'with his forearm he gathers the lambs, with his bosom carries, leads the nurse-mothers.' He [should] remember the hidden, seek the young, heal the broken, sustain the needy and return the lost. And he [should] have mercy on Israel and carry their load with a pleasant countenance - like the Highest Merciful One, who tolerates everything and does not wither nor ignore nor get sick [of them], but [rather] leads each one according to his need.

These are the traits of Wisdom, the merciful Father over [Its] children.

To have mercy upon all of the creatures:

He must also have his mercy extend to all the creatures. He [should] not disgrace them nor destroy them. As behold, the Highest Wisdom is spread over all the creatures - the inanimate, the growing (plants), the living (animals) and the speaking (people). And we are warned about disgracing food for this reason. And about this thing it is fitting that [just] like the Highest Wisdom does not disgrace anything in existence and everything was made from There, as it is written, "You made all of them with wisdom" - so [too, should] the mercy of a person be over all of His creations, may He be blessed. And for this reason, was the holy Rebbe punished: Since he did not pity the young calf that was hiding with him and said to it, "Go, you were created for this," afflictions came upon him (Bava Metzia 85a). As they were from the side of judgement; since behold, mercy protects from judgement. And when he had mercy on a weasel and said, "It is written (Psalms 145:9), 'and His mercies are over all of His creatures,'" he was saved from the judgement - since the light of Wisdom was spread over him and the afflictions withdrew. And upon this way, he [should] not disgrace anything in existence from that which exists, as all of them are with Wisdom. And [so] he [should] not uproot a plant except for a need nor kill an animal except for a need. And [then] he [should] chose a nice death, with a checked knife, to have mercy in as much as is possible.

This is the general rule:

Compassion upon all things in existence - not to injure them - is [rooted] in Wisdom. [This is] unless it is to raise them from [one] level to [another] level - from growing to living; from living to speaking. As then it is permitted to uproot a [plant] and kill an [animal] - to disadvantage [it] in order to benefit [it].

TOMER Chapter Three DEVORAH

Sefer Tomer Devorah

Chapter Four

How a person can accustom himself with the trait of understanding (binah):

Understanding is repentance. And this is that one [should] repent - as there is nothing as important as it, since it repairs every defect. And like it is the way of Understanding to sweeten all of the judgments and to nullify their bitterness, so [should] a person repents and fix every defect. And one who ponders repentance all of his day's causes Understanding to shine upon him all of his days. 'And it comes out that all of his days are in repentance' - which is [to say that he] is including himself in Understanding, which is Repentance. And [so] the days of his life are crowned with the secret of the Highest Repentance. And see, that [just] like Repentance has the root of all that is in existence in it through the secret of the Jubilee, and behold the root of the external forces - [which] is the secret of the River Dinur which is included in the holiness of the secret of the severities - is [also] rooted There and extends from There and this extension is called the extension of the burning fury, but the extension returns to its Source in the secret of "And the Lord smelled the pleasant smell" (Genesis 8:21), and the judgments are sweetened and the fury is stilled, 'and the Lord relents of the evil'; so [too] does a person do this secret with the secret of his repentance.

Repentance is also good for the bad, that you [should] not say that repentance is only good for the holy part in man - but rather it also sweetens the evil part in him, similar to this [Higher] trait:

Know that Kain was bad and was from the snake, but it was stated to him (Genesis 4:7), "Is it not that if you do good, it will be lifted" - do not think that because you are from the side of evil, that you have no reparation; that is a lie! Is it not that "if you do good" and root yourself in the secret of repentance, "it will be lifted," [such] that you will withdraw to there in the secret of the good rooted there - as all the Highest Bitterness has a sweet root and can enter through its root to better itself. And so, these same actions improve a person, and his 'volitional sins are made for him [to be] like merits." As behold, those actions that he did were prosecuting from the 'left side.' [If] he repented with complete repentance, behold, he brings these actions in and roots them to the Above. And all of these prosecutors do not become nullified, but rather improve themselves and root themselves in holiness, similar to the [possible] betterment of Kain. And behold, if Kain had repented and been repaired; behold, the volitional sin of Adam (literally the first man) through which he fathered Kain - who is the nest (kina) of impurity - would have been considered a merit, through the secret of 'a child gives merit to the father' (Sanhedrin 104a). However, he did not want to repent. And hence, all the 'side of the left' is drawn from there. But all of its branches are destined to be sweetened, and they will repent and be sweetened. And this is exactly from the reason that we explained - that a person takes the secret of evil to his own roots and sweetens it and brings it into the good. Hence, a person purifies his evil impulse and brings it into the good, and it becomes rooted in holiness Above.

And this is the virtue of repentance that a person practice. He must ponder it each and every day and repent in some way, so that 'all of his days will be in repentance.'

Sefer Tomer Devorah

Chapter Five

How a person can accustom himself with the trait of kindness (chese"d):

Its essence is love of God - the main entrance for a person to the secret of kindness is to love God with the fullest love, such that he will not leave His service for any reason. [This is] on account of there being nothing at all as beloved to him, relative to his love of Him, may He be blessed. And so, he [should] first fix all the needs of His service; and what remains afterwards will be for other needs. And this love [should] be fixed in his heart. Whether he receives goodnesses from the Holy One, blessed be He, or whether he receives afflictions and upbraidings, he [should] consider them [to be products of His] love for him, as it is written (Proverbs 27:6), "Faithful are the wounds of a friend." And it is as it is [also] written (Deuteronomy 6:5), "and with all your might (meodecah)" - and they explained (Berakhot 54a), "With each and every trait (midah), etc., so as to include all of the traits in Kindness. And it comes out that the secret of His governance is from Kingship (Malkhut); and even as it acts with judgement, it is connected to Kindness. And this is the trait of Nachum, the man of Gamzo, who would say, "This too (Gam zo) is for the good." He wanted to always connect [occurrences] to the side of Kindness that is called good, and [so] he would say, "This too," that appears to be with the 'left' that is connected to Severity (Gevurah), "is" nothing but "for the good," [which is] connected to Kindness. And he would put his mind to the side of the good with this trait and hide its judgments. And this is a great practice, always to connect with Kindness.

And in the Tikkunim (in the Introduction), they explained, "Who is pious one (chasid)? One who is kindly (mitchased) with his Maker." [That is] since a person must intend, in the acts of kindness that he does with the lower ones (other people), the Highest reparation that is its model - and that is bestowing Kindness with his Maker.

From kindness with people, one learns kindness with one's Creator:

And now, he needs to know how many are the traits of acts of kindness with people. And he [should] do all of them with his Creator, if he wants to acquire the trait of kindness. And so, we shall say that the traits of acts of kindness are these:

The first: When a person is born, every arrangement for his nourishment must be provided for him. If so, he should call up to his mind the giving birth of Understanding [to] Splendor (Tiferet). And it is that in Its difficulty in Its birth from the angle of judgement, God forbid, Splendor comes out to the side of the severities and Its birth [would be] in difficulty (hardness); [hence] there is a need to fix all that is possible there - that the birth of Splendor be to the 'right side,' so that the Offspring be without blemish at all. [It is] as we say, "And bring our judgement out to the light, Holy one" - which is that He take out Splendor [which is] judgement to the side of the light, which is the right, and It will [then] be holy and separated from the severities. And in this is included his having in mind in his actions to always connect [his action] with Kindness, to have It come out from Understanding to the side of Kindness. And then the Offspring will come out vital and lustrous. And almost every warning in the Torah is included in this; so that the severities not arouse intensification of the judgments there, and there not be difficulty in Its birth, God forbid.

The second: To circumcise the offspring - that is to do [it] according to the refinements of its commandments. That he [should] circumcise any husk (klipah) and foreskin that is attached to the Foundation (Yesod), chase all those that cause foreskin There and bring them to repentance in a way that in his circumcising the foreskin of their hearts, the Highest Righteous One will be without a foreskin. And he [should] stand strongly to fix all of the things that cause foreskin There. And so when Pinchas circumcised the foreskin of the Children of Israel, he merited priesthood. Since he bestowed kindness [to] his Maker with the secret of circumcision - that he circumcised the Foundation from that foreskin - he merited kindness. And so, from this, one should learn to all the other traits of kindness.

The third: To visit the sick and to heal them. It is thus known that the Divine Presence is lovesick for unification, as it is written (Song of Songs 2:5), "for I am sick with love." And Her healing is in the hand of man, to bring Her proper drugs, as it is written, "Support me with fruitcakes, lay apples below me." And they explained in the Tikkunim (p. 39b) that the secret of fruitcakes (ashishot) is all of the things that are connected to Kingship (Malkhut) - through the man (eesh) [that includes the letter,] hay (five, which is) Kindness, and through the woman (eeshah) [that includes the letter,] yod (ten, which is) Severity, [which] is through the two forearms. And She supports Herself upon them there. And whoever does this supports the patient in his sickness.

The explanation of the second [phrase], "lay apples below me" is to connect Her between Victory (Netsach) and Majesty (Hod). As Her couch is there, in Her being white and red - like those apples the colors of which are mixed - from the side of Kindness. And he needs to visit Her, remember Her and to beseech Her countenance, that She accept food and drink from the Highest flow, which She prevents from Herself and [accordingly] makes Her soul pine for the travail of Israel. In the way that it is with physical patients, so is it with Highest Patients, as She is sick, like we said. And He is [also] sick, as He is 'wandering' from His place - the world to come, Understanding - 'and roaming' from Her in this World; as it is written (Proverbs 27:8), "As a bird roaming from its nest" - which is the Divine Presence - "so is a man roaming from his place." And He waits for Her and swears to her that He will not return to His place until He brings Her back to Her place. Behold, He is also 'wounded because of our sins, willingly crushed because of our iniquities.' And the healing of both of Them is in our hands. And it is fitting to visit Them and to procure Their needs through Torah [study] and through [fulfillment of] the commandments.

The fourth: To give charity (tsedekah) to the poor, the model of whom is Foundation and Kingship. And they have explained in the Tikkunim (Tikkun 18, p. 33a) that the charity that is fit for Them is to every day implement ninety [recitations of] amen, four [of] kedushah, one hundred blessings and five books of the Torah (as these numbers corresponds to the letters that spell out the word, tsedekah). And in this way, everyone [should] draw charity from Splendor to these Poor Ones. And he [should] procure for Them gleanings from all of the Sefirot, forgotten sheaves from the secret of the Highest Sheaf - which is Understanding - and the corner from the aspect of Kingship itself, as it is the corner for the other traits (it is the outermost Sefirah). It is written (Leviticus 19:10), "for the poor and the stranger shall you leave them" - as even Splendor is a stranger [when it is] below in Kingship, and one must give It from these reparations. And so [too, must one give] the poor tithe, to bring up Kingship, which is Tithe, to the Foundation, which is called the Poor. And if he connects it with Splendor, he will give from the Tithe to the Stranger. And several reparations are included in this.

The fifth: Bringing in guests. [The guests] are Splendor and Foundation - to give them a house for resting, such that they rest there, meaning in Kingship. Since They are Wayfarers in the secret of the exile - to search for Their lost object - he must bring Them in there. And according to what is elucidated in the Zohar, Vayera 1:115b, this commandment is implemented by those who are 'wayfarers that speak'; which are those expelled from their houses to be involved in Torah [study], who cause that the Guests will be involved in the needs of Kingship. And so [too,] anyone who creates a unification for Splendor in Kingship from another aspect and fixes a place for his Torah [study], causes Splendor to make its residence in Kingship. And so, did they explain in the Tikkunim (in the Introduction). And one must prepare food, drink and escort for the Guests. That is that one must bring in Splendor and Foundation to Kingship; give them food, similar to, "I have come to my garden, I have eaten my honeycombs and my honey" (Song of Songs 5:1), which is the flow that is fitting for the lower governance that extends from the side of the sweetened Severity; and drink, similar to "I have drunken my wine with my milk,' which is the inner flow from the wine that is guarded, and from the secret of the milk sweetened to connect Splendor and Kingship - [which are] Yaakov and Rachel - and Severity with Victory or with Majesty. As so did they explain in the Raaya Meheimena (Vayikra, p. 4b). And the escort is to bring himself and his soul There with Them in their Highest Replication, to escort Them There; also, to bring the other Sefirot There with Them to make a good escort for Them. And there are several things included in this reparation.

The general principle of the thing is that he make efforts about the needs of the commoner (a person) and have intention for its allusion. And

[so] he can be assured that Above will be done similar to [what he is doing], once he is an expert in the secrets. And how good is it to mention the allusion of his intention with his mouth at the time of the deed, to fulfill "in your mouth and in your heart to do it" (Deuteronomy 30:14)!

The sixth: The dealing of the living with the dead. And how this thing relates to the Above is very difficult, as it is secret of the Sefirot, that become hidden and withdraw into Their containers above. How much must one repair Them to wash Them from every sickness of iniquity; to clothe Them in white - the whitening of the Sefirot in the light of the good deed - to have Them rise up in the secret of one; to connect Them above; and to carry Them on the shoulder, [which is] the secret of the raising of the Sefirot, One by One, until they are risen up over the Shoulder which is the beginning of the joining of the Forearm with the Body. But above this is the secret of hiding, about which there is no comprehension. And about the secret of burial, he should have intention for the verse (Deuteronomy 34:6), "And He buried him in the valley (gai)," which we translate [into Aramaic], "with thirteen crowns of mercy" (as the numerical equivalent of gai is thirteen). As they emerge from the Crown from its aspects that face downwards to have mercy on the Ones below. And from there the buried, rises to the Highest Eden - Wisdom in the Crown. And there is a need for much concentration in this.

The seventh: Bringing a bride under the canopy. And all of the needs of unification are included in this, as all of the prayers and the unifications are the secret of bringing a bride under the canopy. And its essence is the secret of prayer of several levels, this after that - the [recital of the] sacrifices; the [songs]; the sitting prayer in which there is the recital of Shema and its blessings; the standing prayer afterwards; and the rest of the reparations that come after them. It is all the bestowal of kindness upon the Groom and the Bride, to supervise all of Their needs and the reparations of Their pairing.

The eighth: The bringing of peace between a man and his fellow, which are Splendor and Foundation. Sometimes, They become distant One from the Other, and there is a need to bring peace between Them and to repair Them, that They be parallel and connected together in love and amity. And this [happens] through the propriety of the good deed. As when Foundation inclines to the left and Splendor to the right, They are then in opposition One to the Other - until Foundation inclines to the right like [Splendor has]. But when there is, God forbid, a defect of iniquity in the world, then there is hatred and opposition between the two of Them, and unification among the Sefirot is not connected at all. And in this way is it also between all the [pairs] of Sefirot that are right and left: between Wisdom and Understanding; between Kindness and Severity; and between Victory and Majesty - one needs to bring peace (a middle Sefirah) between Them, and that is [the meaning of] the bringing of peace between a Man and his Fellow. And likewise, between a Man and His Wife is that the Foundation is peace between Splendor and Kingship. And everything that is similar to this in the ways of peace is [accounted as] acts of kindness Above.

TOMER   Chapter Five   DEVORAH

Sefer Tomer Devorah

Chapter Six

How a person can accustom himself with the trait of severity (gevura"h):

Know that all actions of the arousal of the evil impulse truly arouse the strong severities. Hence, he should not activate his evil impulse, so that he not arouses Severity. And the explanation is that a man is created with two impulses - the good impulse and the evil impulse, this is Kindness and that is Severity. However, they explained in the Zohar in Parshat Bereishit (p. 49a) that the good impulse was created for the man himself for his need, and the evil impulse was crated for the need of his wife. See how sweet are its words - Splendor, which is the husband of Kindness inclines to the right; and all of His actions are with the right, the good impulse. And the Female

(Kingship) is to the left and all of Its actions are with Severity. If so, it is fitting not to arouse the evil impulse for his own sake; as he so arouses the Highest Man in Severity and destroys the world. If so, any traits that a man arouses for himself that are from the side of severity harms the Highest Man. And from this, he should see how disgraceful anger and anything like it is - as it intensifies the harsh severities. Indeed, the evil impulse must be tied and bound, that it not arouses any action in the world, from the actions of his body - not for the desire for intercourse, nor for the desire for money, and not from the angle of anger and the angle of honor at all.

However, for the need of his wife, he [should] gently arouse his [evil] impulse from the side of the sweetened severities, such as to clothe her [and] to arrange a house for her. And he [should] say, "Behold, with that which I am clothing [my wife], I am repairing the Divine Presence" - as it is adorned by Understanding, which is Severity that contains all of the severities, but they are sweetened by Her many mercies. Hence, all the arrangements of the house are arrangements (reparations) of the Divine Presence, which is sweetened from the evil impulse that was created to do the will of its Maker and nothing else. Hence, a man [should] not intend any pleasure of anything for himself; but when his wife enjoys a pleasant residence [from] him, he [should] intend [it] for the reparation of the Divine Presence which is repaired by the good severities of the left, from which there is wealth and honor. And from this angle, he [should] arouse his evil impulse for Her love, and then intend towards the left that is aroused, to bring it close with the secret of "His left is under my head" (Song of Songs 8:3): At first, he only connects from the side of the left, and afterwards - "and with his right, he embraces me" - he [should] intend to sweeten all of those reparations with his good impulse and to actually repair Her, to have Her rejoice in the matter of a commandment for the sake of the Highest unification. Behold, he [thus] sweetens all of the severities and repairs them with the right. And in this way [should] all desires coming from the side of the evil impulse be primarily for the arrangements of his wife, whom God has shown to him to be his helpmate. And he [should] transform all of them afterwards to the service of God, to connect them with the right [side].

Sefer Tomer Devorah

Chapter Seven

How a person can accustom himself with the trait of splendor (tifere"t):

There is no doubt that the trait of splendor is involvement in Torah. However, a person needs great care not to become haughty with words of Torah, that he not cause great evil. As behold, [just] like he becomes haughty, so does he cause the trait of Splendor - which is the Torah - to become haughty and withdraw Above, God forbid. Rather anyone that lowers himself with words of Torah causes Splendor to descend and lower itself, to flow to Kingship. And behold, there are four Sefirot below Splendor and they have three traits.

The first: One who becomes haughty over his students causes Splendor to be haughty and rise above Victory and Majesty, which are 'Those taught of God' - the Students of Splendor. But one who lowers himself and teaches it with love, [brings that] Splendor will also lower Itself towards Its Students and teach Them, according to what They can carry. And in his merit, Splendor will flow upon 'Those taught of God' according to Their aspect that is fitting for them.

The second: One who makes himself haughty with his Torah over the poor person, like that occurrence of Eliyahu who appeared to Rabbi Shimon ben Elazar like an ugly disgraced and disgusting poor man (Taanit 20a), in order to make him stumble. As his head had swelled [from his Torah knowledge] and he disgraced the poor man, and [so Eliyahu] rebuked him for his blemish. As one who is haughty over the poor, causes Splendor to be haughty over Foundation and not to flow upon It. But if the mind of the sage is settled [in his dealings] with the poor person, then Splendor will flow onto Foundation. Hence a poor person should be very important to the sage, and he should bring him close; and so will Foundation be considered above to Splendor and [the Latter] will connect with [the Former].

The third: One who becomes haughty from his Torah upon the people of the land - which is the general people of God - causes Splendor to become haughty over Kingship and not to flow upon it. Rather, his disposition [should] be pleasant with the creatures and all the people of the settlement be important in front of him - as they are below in the secret of the Land. And God forbid, if he calls them donkeys, he lowers them to the husks. Hence, he will not merit to have a son that will have the light of the Torah in him, as it is [found] in the Gemara (Nedarim 81a). Rather, he should behave with them gently, according to their way, similar to Splendor that flows to Kingship and guides Her according to the poverty of Her mind - as the 'minds of women are weak" (Shabbat 33b). And included in this is that he not become haughty over the weak of mind that are included in the 'dust of the earth.' And because of this, the ancient ones would not become haughty from their Torah, like [in] that occurrence of Rav

Hamnuna in [the Zohar,] Parshat Bereishit and like the occurrence of Rabbi Chagai (Zohar, Part I, p. 158a), and in the Tikkunim (the end of Tikkun 26, p. 72b) of that elder who fled when they wanted to kiss him, as he did not want to become haughty with words of Torah.

He should also be accustomed in his going back and forth (his discussion and argument) in the words of Torah to intend the reparation of the Divine Presence, to repair It and adorn It to Splendor - which is the Law to the Truth. And this is [the meaning of] a 'disagreement for the sake of the Heavens' - which is [for] Kindness and Severity to come to Splendor, the Heavens - to have the Law correspond to It. And he [should] separate from any disagreement that goes out of this line, as Splendor will not want to grasp what is outside, even if it be with words of Torah. If it is [just] to argue, its end will be Geihinom, God forbid. And you have no disagreement that does not harm Splendor besides a disagreement of the Torah for the sake of the Heavens - as 'all of its paths are peace' and love is at its end.

And one who consumes pleasures from the words of Torah hurts this trait, as it is holy and he [makes] it words of the mundane. But when one is involved in words of Torah for the pleasure of the Higher Realm, happy is his portion. And the essence of everything is to refine his mind through the aspect of thought, and to examine himself by way of give and take. If there be found a trace of an improper thing, he [should] go back on it; and he [should] always concede to the truth, so that Splendor - the trait of Truth - will be found there.

TOMER   Chapter Seven   DEVORAH

Sefer Tomer Devorah

Chapter Eight

How a person can accustom himself with the traits of victory (netsac"h), majesty (ho"d) and foundation (yeso"d):

The reparations of Victory, Majesty in Their Commonality - [as with] the reparations of Victory and Majesty, some of them are common to both of them and some of them are unique, each one to itself - [are as follows].

And behold, first he must assist those that study Torah, and to strengthen them - whether with his money or his actions - to provide the requirements that they will use, the provision of food and the supply of all that they want, so that they not desist from the words of Torah; and to be careful not to disgrace their study, that they not be weakened from [their] occupation with

Torah, but rather to honor them and to praise their good deeds, in order to strengthen them in their service; and to provide them with books required for their occupation and a study hall, and all that is similar [to it] - which is for strengthening and assistance to those occupied with Torah. It is all dependent on these two traits (victory and majesty) - everyone according to his ability, whether it is little or much. In the end, all that he can increase in this to honor the Torah and to strengthen it - with [his] speech, with his body, and with his means - and to stimulate the hearts of the creatures to the Torah, that they should be strengthened in it; it is all held and rooted in these two Sefirot, in that they are called Those that hold it and its Supporters.

One occupied with the Torah must also learn from every person, as it is written (Psalms 119:99), "From all of my teachers have I been enlightened." As the Torah is not completed with one teacher; but since he becomes a student to all, he merits to become a chariot for Victory and Majesty, 'Those taught of God'; and the one who bestows Torah upon him is on the level of Splendor. And behold, in his sitting and studying Torah, he merits that Splendor flows on Victory and Majesty and [that] he actually be on Their level.

Victory and Majesty individually:

And behold, in his studying Scripture which is from the right, he has a connection to Victory individually; and in his studying Mishnah which is from the left, he has a connection to Majesty individually. And behold, the Gemara that is included in everything - such that it brings a proof to the laws of the Mishnah from the verse - is a reparation for both of Them together.

The reparations of the foundation:

How does a man, however, accustom himself to the trait of foundation? He must be very careful from speech that brings lustful thought, so that he not come to a nocturnal emission. There is no need to say that he [should] not speak a vile thing, but it is fitting to guard even from a pure thing that brings to a lustful thought. And so was the expression of the verse exacting (Ecclesiastes 5:5), "Do not let your mouth make your flesh sin" - it warned that he not allow his mouth speech that brings his holy flesh - the sign of the covenant (circumcision) - to sin, with an accidental emission. And it is written [further], "why should God be angered, etc." - and if it was [speaking] about vile [speech], what is [the meaning of] "to make sin"; behold, it is a sin itself? Rather, even if the speech is not a sin but only a pure thing - if it brings to lustful thought, he should be careful from it. And that is why it stated, "to make your flesh sin, why should [He] be angered" - it means [to say], since it brings to sin, He will be angry about that voice, even though it is permitted. As since an evil act ensued from it, the voice and speech became evil. This much carefulness must there be about the sign of the covenant, to not have lustful thoughts and not be destructive.

And he must also be careful as Foundation is the sign of the covenant of the rainbow. And the Bow is only drawn Above to send arrows to the trait of Kingship; and it guards the drop that shoots like an arrow 'to make a branch and carry a fruit.' And just like the Highest Bow never draws except across from the mentioned target - so should a man never draw the bow and not make himself have an erection in any way except for across from the fitting target. [And that] is his wife [when] she is in her [time] of purity, which is the time of mating. And not more than this, which would harm this trait, God forbid. And one needs much, much carefulness - and the main carefulness is that he guards himself from lustful thought.

Chapter Eight

Sefer Tomer Devorah

Chapter Nine

How a person can accustom himself with the trait of kingship (malkhu"t):

To lower himself - that his heart not become haughty, he [should] first of all always make himself like a poor person in front of his Maker, like an indigent requesting and begging. To accustom himself to this trait - even if he is rich - he [should] think that there is not a thing that is attached to him from all that he has; and he [is] forsaken and always needs the mercy of the Creator, since he has nothing besides the bread that he eats. And he [should] subdue his heart and afflict himself. And even more so at the time of his prayers, as it is a wonderful device. And [about] the opposite of this is it stated (Deuteronomy 8:14), "And your heart will rise and you will forget" - as external forgetfulness is found there. And David supplicated with this trait much, as he stated (Psalms 25:16), "for I am alone and poor." As behold, each and every one of the people of his household needs to help himself - what are they [then] to him? And even his wife and children, what will they help him when he is judged in front of the Creator or at the time that his soul is withdrawn? Will they accompany him any [further] than to his grave? What are they for him at the time of his judgments from the opening of the grave and beyond? Hence, he [should] lower and refine himself with the secret of this trait.

To go into exile:

There is a second [method] that they explained in the Book of the Zohar (Vayekhel, 198b) and it is very important - that he [should] exile himself from place to place for the sake of the Heavens. And through this, he will become a chariot for the exiled Divine Presence. And he [should] compare himself, "Behold I am in exile and behold I have all of the vessels [that I need] with me; what does the honor of the Higher Realm do, as the Divine Presence was exiled, but her vessels are not with Her - as they were removed on account of the exile?" And so, he [should] minimize his vessels with all of his ability, as it is written (Jeremiah 46:19), "Vessels of an exile make for yourself." And he [should] subdue his heart in the exile and connect to Torah; and then the Divine Presence will be with him. And he [should] make for himself an expulsion, and always expel himself from the house of his resting, in the way that Rabbi Shimon and his colleagues would expel themselves and occupy themselves with Torah. And all the more so if he can pound his feet from place to place without a horse and wagon. About [such a one] is it stated (Psalms 146:5), "his hope (sivro) is to the Lord, his God" - and they explained (Zohar, Vayekhel, 198a) about it, that it is an expression of breaking (shever) - such that he breaks his body for the honor of the Higher Realm.

To fear God:

There is another very important trait from the trait of kingship [and it is] the gateway to all [Divine] service, and that is to fear the glorious and awesome God. And behold, fear is very much in danger of being harmed and that the external forces enter it. As behold, if he fears from afflictions, from death or from Geihinom - observe that this is fear of the external forces, since all of these functions are from the external forces. However, the essential fear is to fear God - and that is that he thinks about three things:

The first:

That the greatness of the Creator of all is over all that exists.

And behold a man fears from a lion, from a bear, from a violent man, from fire, from a falling structure and yet they are small agents. And [so] why would he not fear from the great King, [such that] His fear be on his face from His greatness. And he [should] say, "How can a disgraceful man sin to a big Master like this? And behold, [is it] because if He were a bear, He would eat him, whereas the Holy One, blessed be He, [actually] tolerates the insult, that he does not fear from His awe and His greatness?"

The second:

When he envisions His constant supervision, [such] that He watches and observes him.

And behold, the slave always fears from his master when he is in front of him. And a person is always in front of the Creator, and His eye is open upon all of his ways - he [should] fear and be afraid, how He can see him negate His commandments.

The third:

His being the Source of all the souls.

And they are all rooted in His Sefirot. And [so] the sinner harms His chamber. And why does he not fear how the chamber of the King is dirty from his bad deeds?

The fourth:

His fear that the defect of his deeds are pushing the Divine Presence from Above.

And he [should] fear how he causes this great evil, to break off the desire of the King from the Queen. And the fear that is similar to this is the fear that straightens a person to the reparation of this trait. And he [should] cling to it.

To make it that the Divine Presence clings to him by his behavior with his wife:

There is also much care that a man must take for himself [in this] to make it that the Divine Presence be clinging to him and not separate from him. And behold, it is obvious that when a man has not yet married a woman, the Divine Presence is not with him at all; as the essence of the Divine Presence for a man is from the side of the female. And a man stands between the two females - the lower physical female, who takes 'flesh, covering and time' from him; and the Divine Presence that stands above him, to bless him with all of them, that he give and give again to the wife of his covenant. [This is] like the matter of Splendor that stands between two Females - the Higher Mother (Understanding) that flows all that is needed to Him; and the Lower Mother (Kingship), [that] receives from Him, 'flesh, covering and time,' which are Kindness, judgement (Severity) and mercy (Splendor), as is known. And the Divine Presence will not come to him if he does not resemble the Highest Existence.

Behold, sometimes a man separates from his wife for one of three reasons:

The first - in her being a menstruant.

The second - in his being occupied with Torah and separating from her all of the weekdays.

The third - in his going on the way and guarding himself from sin.

And at these times, the Divine Presence is clinging and bound to him and It does not leave him, so that he not be abandoned and separated. Rather the man is always complete, male and female. And behold [since] the Divine Presence is coupled with him when he goes out on the way, a man must be careful that It not separate from him. And he [should] be alacritous and rewarded to pray the prayer of the way and to hold on to Torah. As from this reason, the Divine Presence - which is Protection of the way - always stands for him; in that he is being careful from sin and occupied with Torah. And so [too,] when his wife is a menstruant, the Divine Present stands upon him - when he observes [the laws of] the menstruant as is fitting. Afterwards on the night of her purity, on the Shabbat night or on his coming back from the way - each one of them is a time of commanded intercourse. And the Divine Presence above opens to accept holy souls; so is his wife fitting to visit her. And with this, the Divine Presence is always with him. So is it explained in the Zohar in Parshat Bereishit (p. 49a). The visiting of his wife must be specifically at the time that the Divine Presence is between the two Forearms (Kindness and Severity).

However, at a time that the Divine Presence is not between the two Forearms, it is forbidden. And so is it explained in the Tikkunim, Parshat Bereishit (Tikkun 69).

To repair all of the traits and to accept the yoke of the commandments:

One who wants to be coupled with the Daughter of the King and that She not separate from him ever, must first adorn himself with all types of adornments and nice garments, and they are the reparations of all the traits mentioned. And after he has repaired himself with the reparations, he should intend to receive Her upon himself - in his being occupied with Torah and always carrying the yoke of the commandments in the secret of intention for unification. And [then] immediately, she marries him and does not separate from him. And this is on condition that he purifies and sanctifies himself. And after he is pure and holy, he should have in mind to fulfill for Her, 'flesh, covering and time' which a man is obligated [to give] to his wife.

The first:

To bestow upon Her a flow from the right with all of his deeds - Her nourishment.

The second:

To cover Her from the side of Severity. That the external forces not rule [over] Her, such that there not be a side of the evil impulse in his involvement with the commandments - such as pleasure to the body, or hoping for illusory honor, and similar to it. As the evil impulse is [then] found in that commandment; and She flees from it, because it is 'nakedness.' If so, he must cover the nakedness, to always hide it that it should not rule [over] Her. How is that? All of his deeds [should be] for the sake of the Heavens, without any portion for the evil impulse. And so [too,] tefillin and tsitsit are great protections for Her, such that the external forces not rule [over] Her. And he [should] be accustomed to [wearing] them.

The third:

To unify Her with Splendor at the time of the Recital of Shema and in the setting of time for Torah [study]. And when he sets a time for anything, he [should] have in mind that this is the set time of the Divine Presence, the Daughter of the King. And there is a hint to this in the Tikkunim.

TOMER   Chapter Nine   DEVORAH

Sefer Tomer Devorah

Chapter Ten

To connect with the Sefirot according to the time period:

Rabbi Shimon explained in [the Zohar,] Parshat Bereishit (p. 11a) a big and great counsel from the Torah, how a person is to connect to the Highest Holiness, act with It, and never separate from the Highest Sefirot. And in it, a man must act according to the time; meaning to say to know what Sefirah is ruling [at that time], connect to it and do the reparation that relates to the trait that is [therefore] ruling.

At night he [should] connect with Kingship:

And he begins from the night, at the time that a man lays down on his bed. And behold the rulership is to Night, the trait of Kingship. And he goes to sleep - and sleep is similar to death, and the tree of death rules. What shall he do? He [should] repair and precede to connect to the secret of holiness, which is the secret of the trait of kingship, from the aspect of its holiness. And so he [should] go on his bed and accept the full yoke of the Kingship of the Heavens with concentration of the heart. He gets up at midnight, [washes] his hands from the husk that is governing them, removes the evil from his flesh and recites a blessing. And he [should] repair the Divine Presence through the occupation with Torah. And about this is it stated (Proverbs 6:22), "When you lie down it will watch over you," from the external forces; "and when you awake, it will talk with you." And She will be connected to him, and he to Her. And the likeness of his soul will rise in the Garden of Eden with the Divine Presence that is entering there with the righteous ones. And Splendor will also come there to play with the righteous ones, and with him in their company - as they will all be listening to his voice. Behold, he has actually traveled with Her from death and sleep to the secret of the Garden of Eden and began to cause the light of Splendor, that sparkles in the Garden of Eden upon the righteous, to sparkle upon him. And so is it explained in [the Zohar,] Parshat Terumah (p. 130b).

In the morning, he [should] connect himself to the traits of the three fathers that are included in Splendor:

When the dawn rises, he also begins to come to the synagogue and bind himself to the three fathers. At the opening of the synagogue, he says, "But I, through Your abundant kindness, enter, etc." (Psalms 5:8). And he includes himself in the secret of the Splendor of Man that includes Kindness, Severity and Splendor, and he enters the assembly of Kingship.

And he has intention in the verse for the three fathers:

"Through Your abundant kindness" - that is Avraham.

"I bow down at Your holy chamber" - that is Yitschak, as bowing down, to bend one's stature across from the trait of judgment (Severity) to be pushed off before it, is from his side. And then the time [of pain] is pushed off in front of him, as a flow of mercy is pulled towards it from Above to sweeten it.

"In Your awe" - that is Yaakov, as about him is it written (Genesis 28:17), "how awesome is this place."

And behold, he has included himself in Them in thought, speech and deed: As the thought that we mentioned is the intention; the speech is the verse; and the deed is the entering into the synagogue and his bowing down across from His chamber.

The traits to which he connects during the course of the day:

Before prayer he stands in the synagogue. His mouth exudes prayer and the unification of Foundation - the Source of the well (Foundation) opens up in the well, which is the synagogue (Kingship) - and he repairs the Divine Presence with all the power of the intention of his prayer. He leaves from there and rises to the secret of Torah, and connects to it in the secret of the measure of day; and he is involved with it all of the day until the time of the afternoon prayer, when he connects to Severity. As behold, in the morning, he was connected to Kindness in his prayer, and in the day to Splendor in occupation in Torah; and [so] in the evening, [is it] with Severity. And all of this is in the measure of the day - that he comes to the synagogue to unify with the secret of Severity, in the way that he did from the side of Kindness.

And between this and that, he connects the Divine Presence to him in his meal, such that he bestows kindness on the poor one - as Hillel the Elder (Vayikra Rabbah 34:3) would say, "A righteous one should know the soul of his animal" (Proverbs 12:10). And this [should] be his intention in his meal, to bestow kindness to the animal soul and to connect it with the secret of nourishment.

And after he arrived to the time of the afternoon prayer and he connected with Severity, he waits to the evening and Splendor goes down to Kingship. And behold, he is with [Splendor] at the beginning of the night, connects himself with It and enters the synagogue with the intention mentioned above and he connects himself Below - [so] Splendor comes to the House of Its lodging.

He exits the synagogue [and] unifies himself truly with Kingship alone, through the secret of accepting the yoke of the Kingdom of the Heavens. And this is his strength during the day, with the strength of the Sefirah. And he [should] always cling to the Light that is ruling.

This essence of this counsel is in [the Zohar,] Parshat Bereishit, and the rest is gathered from many places in the Zohar. It is a comprehensive counsel, to always connect a man to holiness; and the crown of the Divine Presence will [thereby] never leave his head.

It is whole and complete - praise to God, who knows all the hidden - today the fourth day of the week, the twelfth day of the month of Marcheshvan, in the year [numerically encoded in the verse], "May my speech be pleasing to Him; I will rejoice in the Lord" (Psalms 104:34).

www.ingramcontent.com/pod-product-compliance
Lightning Source LLC
Chambersburg PA
CBHW070151080526
44586CB00015B/1938